13   K   Ellis

Autumn is Here!

A Cake in the Morn Book

Heidi Pross Gray

For Hazel, Atticus, Sawyer, and Everett

- you make
every day
perfect -

When changing leaves light up the trees, then flutter to the ground...

When little acorns cover the ground, some hopeful to be trees, others an animal snack...

Autumn is here!

When squirrels seem very busy, chattering while they hoard their wintertime feast...

Autumn is here!

When colored mums fill the bushes with their shocking bursts of sunshine...

Autumn is here!

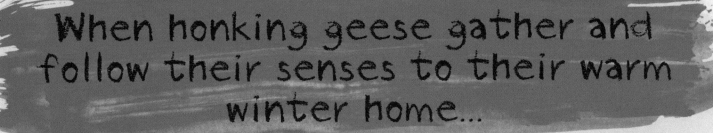

When honking geese gather and follow their senses to their warm winter home...

Autumn is here!

When the apple trees are full and the sweet, crisp fruit is ready to eat...

Autumn is here!

When the kitchen grows warm and the air smells of cinnamon and spice...

Autumn is here!

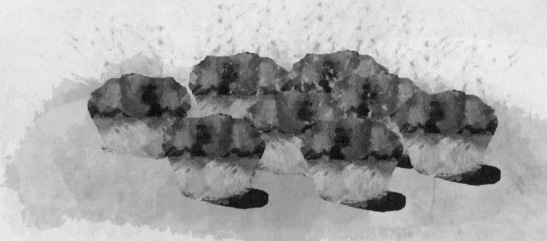

When your fluffy wool hat and your soft woven mittens feel cozy and snug...

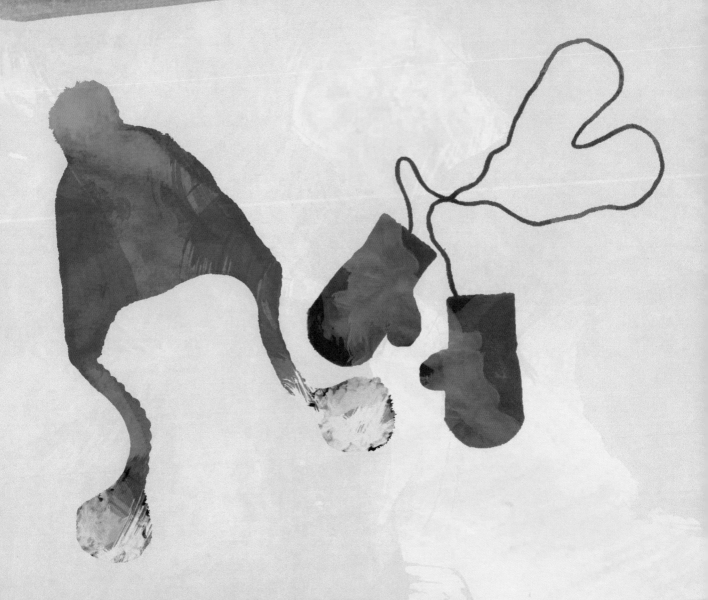

Autumn is here!

When the dry grass is bundled, tied, and scattered in the tractor for a hayride...

Autumn is here!

When pumpkins and gourds litter the fields, waiting to be picked and made into pie...

Autumn is here!

When dancing flames from warm bonfires toast our nighttime treats...

Autumn is here!

When the sun gets sleepy and the moon shines bright, earlier and earlier each day...

Autumn is here!

Active days of traveling, smelling, picking, storing, falling, riding, raking, and playing, bring crisp nights and warm, cozy memories, making autumn a special time of year.

About the Author

Heidi is a mother of four who loves science, reading, and making s'mores by the fire! She loves to read books to her children and anyone else who comes along and wants to join. She can either be found with her kids cooking in the kitchen, sketching an idea on a scratch piece of paper, or outside enjoying nature. Fall is her favorite time of year!

Read all of Heidi's books about the seasons!

Winter is Here!
Spring is Here!
Summer is Here!

To learn more about Heidi and to visit her Montessori toy and book store, visit www.cakeinthemorn.com.

Printed in Great Britain
by Amazon.co.uk, Ltd.,
Marston Gate.